D0320530

THE *Skinny*
BLOOD SUGAR
Diet
RECIPE BOOK

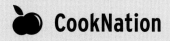

CookNation

THE SKINNY BLOOD SUGAR DIET RECIPE BOOK
DELICIOUS CALORIE COUNTED, LOW CARB RECIPES FOR ONE. THE PERFECT COOKBOOK TO COMPLEMENT YOUR BLOOD SUGAR DIET

Copyright © Bell & Mackenzie Publishing Limited 2016
All rights reserved. This book or any portion thereof may not be reproduced or used in any manner whatsoever without the express written permission of the publisher.

ISBN 978-1-911219-21-7

DISCLAIMER

This book is designed to provide information on meals that can be made in line with the principals of the Blood Sugar Diet.
Some recipes may contain nuts or traces of nuts. Those suffering from any allergies associated with nuts should avoid any recipes containing nuts or nut based oils.
This information is provided and sold with the knowledge that the publisher and author do not offer any legal or other professional advice. In the case of a need for any such expertise consult with the appropriate professional.
This book does not contain all information available on the subject, and other sources of recipes are available.
Every effort has been made to make this book as accurate as possible. However, there may be typographical and or content errors. Therefore, this book should serve only as a general guide and not as the ultimate source of subject information.
This book contains information that might be dated and is intended only to educate and entertain.
The author and publisher shall have no liability or responsibility to any person or entity regarding any loss or damage incurred, or alleged to have incurred, directly or indirectly, by the information contained in this book.

CONTENTS

SKINNY BLOOD SUGAR DIET DINNER RECIPES   49

SKINNY BLOOD SUGAR DIET DESSERT RECIPES 75

SKINNY BLOOD SUGAR DIET SNACK RECIPES 81

OTHER COOKNATION TITLES 89

You may also enjoy the 5:2 Diet Recipe Books
by  CookNation

INTRODUCTION

Our Skinny Blood Sugar Diet recipes have been written to complement a healthy approach to eating following a low carb, low calorie, Mediterranean approach to cooking.

The Blood Sugar Diet is for anyone who has concerns about their blood sugar levels and wishes to lose weight in a healthy controlled manner and maintain a healthy diet for life. **The Skinny Blood Sugar Diet Recipe Book** is packed with delicious, low carbohydrate, low calorie recipes written in line with the core principals of the **Blood Sugar Diet** created by Michael Mosley. By following our recipes that are low in carbs, sugar and calories, but still balanced and tasty, your blood sugar levels will find an equilibrium that in turn will help you to lose weight.

There are benefits to nearly everyone in following a low carb, no sugar diet however please consult with your doctor before embarking on a restricted calorie eating plan particularly if you have a pre-existing medical condition. We do not advise following our recipes if you are or think you may be pregnant, under 18 years, underweight, diagnosed with type 1 diabetes, old or elderly.

RAISED BLOOD SUGAR LEVELS

A raised blood sugar level is one of the primary causes of the global epidemic that is type 2 diabetes. Abnormal levels of sugar in the blood can also significantly increase the risks of heart disease, stroke, cancer, dementia and speed up the ageing process. Over a period of time a poor diet and little exercise can make your body less sensitive to insulin. Insulin is produced by the pancreas and one of it's main purposes is to bring high blood sugar levels down to the 'normal' range, diverting the energy from the glucose to the parts of the body that need it. For example to your muscles following exercise. If your body does become less sensitive to insulin and therefore blood sugar levels continue to rise, the pancreas continues producing insulin to counteract this BUT instead of being used up as energy it is stored as fat and so the cycle continues.

THE BLOOD SUGAR DIET

You may already have been diagnosed with type 2 diabetes or perhaps you have the condition prediabetes - a precursor for type 2 diabetes, which acknowledges the dangerous build up of blood sugar. You may be lucky enough not to suffer from either of these conditions but have a healthy concern about the dangers of increased levels of blood sugar and wish to lose weight. Michael Mosley's Blood Sugar Diet is a life changing approach to reducing blood sugar levels, reversing diabetes, losing weight and maintaining a healthy diet. His best selling book **The 8 Week Blood Sugar Diet** outlines the research and science that underpins his revolutionary approach to improving our health.

His book not only explains what is wrong with our diet but how it can be dramatically improved following an 8 week low carb, low calorie diet to reduce and bring back blood sugar levels into the normal range resulting in excess weight loss, lower levels of stress, increased energy and if you already suffer from type 2 diabetes you may also be free of medication.

We strongly recommend reading Dr. Mosley's book for an in-depth understanding of the problems of raised blood sugar levels facing millions of us and the low carb, Mediterranean style diet he advises.

Our book **The Skinny Blood Sugar Diet Recipe Book** adheres to the diet principles of the Blood Sugar Diet by Michael Mosley. The recipes have been written to compliment this healthy approach to eating following a low carb, low calorie, Mediterranean approach to cooking. All our recipes are balanced and calorie counted allowing you to use in conjunction with the 8 Week Blood Sugar Diet plan or as an ongoing healthy low carb approach.

THERE ARE 3 APPROACHES TO THE BLOOD SUGAR DIET:

- **800 calorie, low carb Mediterranean 8 week fast.** This is the fastest way to lose weight and reduce blood sugar levels and should be maintained for up to 8 weeks.

- **A modified 5:2 Diet approach:** follow a low carb Mediterranean diet for 5 days a week, 800 calorie fast for 2 days.

- **Low carb, Mediterranean style diet:** a slower and lighter approach. Weight loss and blood sugar levels will take longer to fall but may be more suitable for those who do not wish to fast.

PRINCIPLES OF A MEDITERRANEAN STYLE BLOOD SUGAR DIET PLAN

It is generally accepted, based on research and evidence that the Mediterranean style of eating is beneficial to health.

The diet is centered on the healthy living habits of the populations of those countries bordering the Mediterranean Sea and consists primarily of fresh vegetables, fruits, beans, whole grains, olive oil and fish. Research has shown that adopting a Mediterranean diet can reduce the possibility of developing conditions such as type 2 diabetes, heart disease, obesity, high blood pressure and Alzheimer's disease.

Put simply the Mediterranean Diet is a lifestyle choice. Rather than a strict list of what not to eat, it is a formula for daily healthy living. A low carb approach to Mediterranean style cooking avoids easily digestible processed carbs, which are high in starch and cause blood sugar levels to rise.

Avoid sugar intake – sugary drinks, sweets and desserts should be shunned as much as you can. While fresh fruit is healthy and to be encouraged, avoid too many tropical type fruits such as mango and pineapple which are high in natural sugar – even bananas! Dark berries are great. Honey, dried fruit and fruit smoothies are all processed quickly buy the body into sugar and should be avoided.

Avoid white carbs – white bread, potatoes, pasta and rice are all examples. Brown or wholegrain alternatives are better but beware of added sugar – especially in bread. In our skinny recipes we use healthier slower digesting alternatives such as quinoa, bulgur, brown & wild rice, cauliflower 'rice', legumes (e.g. beans & lentils) and buckwheat.

Avoid all breakfast cereals. It is a common myth that breakfast cereals are a healthy start to the morning. Nearly all are packed with sugar – even the products that are marketed as protein-packed and healthy. Oats are good alternative as they digest slowly keeping you feeling fuller for longer.

Avoid Alcohol – if you are undertaking the 800 calorie fast we recommend you abstain from alcohol altogether during this period. Otherwise a glass (preferably red) with a meal is acceptable.

Keep snacks to a minimum. Snacks are the downfall for most of us when following any kind of reduced calorie diet. Often the first thing we reach for is something quick and easy out of the fridge or cupboard which more often or not is sweet and high in sugar. The sugar rush which follows, while initially rewarding, quickly causes a sugar crash which inevitably makes us want to eat more – it's a slippery slope so avoid snacking where you can. Healthier alternatives include nuts (not salted or coated in honey) or raw fresh veg like celery or carrot sticks. Dark chocolate is also OK in small quantities. Go for at least a 70% cocoa content.

Healthy fats are OK. Much debate has been had lately about the inclusion of full fat and dairy products over low fat alternatives in our diet. Because the Blood Sugar Diet is low in carbs it allows us to eat a higher level of fat. Fat has more calories with 9 cals per gram compared to 4 calories per gram for protein and carbs but remember that a calorie is a measure of energy and our bodies need energy to function otherwise we become lethargic. The advantage to using full fat diary in your diet is that it keeps you feeling fuller for longer because they digest slowly and they do not significantly increase blood sugar levels. Dairy products however should be used in moderation due to their high level of calories. Trans-fats, which appear in processed foods, should be avoided at all costs. For cooking use olive, rapeseed or coconut oil. Unless otherwise stated all our recipes use full fat dairy ingredients.

We hope you enjoy our recipes. Each chapter is divided simply into calorie counted breakfasts, lunches, dinners, desserts and snacks so you can use in conjunction with the 8 week fast, 5:2 fast or long term low carb Mediterranean style approaches as you choose.

ABOUT COOKNATION

CookNation is the leading publisher of innovative and practical recipe books for the modern, health conscious cook.

CookNation titles bring together delicious, easy and practical recipes with their unique approach - easy and delicious, no-nonsense recipes - making cooking for diets and healthy eating fast, simple and fun.

With a range of #1 best-selling titles - from the innovative 'Skinny' calorie-counted series, to the 5:2 Diet Recipes collection - CookNation recipe books prove that 'Diet' can still mean 'Delicious'!

Visit **www.bellmackenzie.com** to browse the full catalogue.

 **CookNation**

THE *Skinny* BLOOD SUGAR *Diet*
RECIPE BOOK

BREAKFAST

MORNING YOGURT

220
calories per serving

Ingredients

- 6 tbsp Greek yogurt
- 1 tsp honey
- 1 tsp green Matcha tea
- 6 walnut halves
- 100g/3½oz strawberries, chopped

Method

1 Combine together the yogurt, honey and matcha tea.

2 Rinse the strawberries, remove the green tops and finely chop, along with the walnuts.

3 Sprinkle both onto the yogurt and serve.

CHEFS NOTE
Try using vanilla yogurt and cut out the honey.

BLUEBERRY PANCAKE

399
calories per serving

Ingredients

- 120ml/½ cup milk
- 1 medium free-range egg
- Pinch of salt
- 50g/2oz buckwheat flour

- 50g/2oz blueberries
- 2 tsp butter
- 1 tbsp Greek yogurt

Method

1 Beat together the milk, egg and salt.

2 Place the buckwheat in another bowl.

3 Gradually add milk mixture to the flour and stir until you get a smooth batter.

4 Add the butter to a hot pan, pour in the mixture and cook for 1-2 minutes on each side, or until golden.

5 Remove from the pan and place to one side while you cook the others.

6 Serve with a dollop of yogurt and the blueberries on top.

CHEFS NOTE
Buckwheat is actually a fruit seed not a cereal grain.

SERVES 1

MUSTARD MUSHROOMS ON RYE

265
calories per
serving

Ingredients

- 2 tsp olive oil
- ½ garlic cloves, crushed
- 2 shallots, sliced
- 125g/5oz mushrooms, sliced
- 2 tsp Dijon mustard
- 2 tbsp crème fraiche
- 1 piece natural rye bread, lightly toasted
- 1 tbsp freshly chopped flat leaf parsley
- Salt & pepper to taste

Method

1 Gently heat the oil in a pan and sauté the onions and garlic for a few minutes. Add the mushrooms and continue cooking for 8-10 minutes or until the mushrooms are soft and cooked through.

2 Stir through the mustard and crème fraiche, combine well and warm through.

3 Pile the creamy mushrooms and onions onto the rye toast and sprinkle with chopped parsley. Season and serve.

CHEFS NOTE
Add a little paprika to the sauce if you wish.

WILTED SPINACH & BREAKFAST EGGS

277 calories per serving

Ingredients

- 1 red pepper, deseeded & sliced
- ½ tsp paprika
- 2 large free-range eggs
- 2 tsp olive oil
- 75g/3oz spinach leaves
- Salt & pepper to taste

Method

1 Break the eggs into a bowl. Add the paprika, a little seasoning and lightly beat with a fork.

2 Gently heat the oil in a frying pan and add the peppers. Sauté for a few minutes until they begin to soften.

3 Add the spinach and allow to wilt for a minute or two. Pour in the beaten eggs and move around the pan until the eggs begin to scramble. As soon as they start to set remove from the heat and serve with lots of black pepper.

CHEFS NOTE
You can turn this into a spicy alternative by adding a little ground chilli, cumin and coriander.

BERRY & CHIA SEED SMOOTHIE

160 calories per serving

Ingredients

- 50g/2oz strawberries
- A small handful of spinach
- 50g/2oz blueberries
- 250ml/1 cup almond milk
- 1 tsp chia seeds
- 1 tbsp Greek yogurt

Method

1 Remove the strawberry tops and any thick stalks from the spinach.

2 Blend all the ingredients together and serve immediately.

CHEFS NOTE
You could also add a handful of ice to this smoothie if you wish.

FETA OMELETTE

330
calories per
serving

Ingredients

- 2 large free-range eggs
- 50g/5oz feta cheese, crumbled
- 1 tsp olive oil

- 1 tbsp freshly chopped chives
- 50g/2oz watercress
- Salt & pepper to taste

Method

1 Lightly beat the eggs with a fork. Season well and add the crumbled feta cheese and chives.

2 Gently heat the oil in a small frying pan and add the omelette mixture. Tilt the pan to ensure the mixture is evenly spread over the base.

3 Cook on a low to medium heat and, when the eggs are set underneath, fold the omelette in half and continue to cook for a further 2 minutes.

4 Serve with the watercress sprinkled all over the top.

CHEFS NOTE
Check the eggs are set underneath by lifting with a fork before folding the omelette in half.

AVOCADO & STRAWBERRY SALAD

310 calories per serving

Ingredients

- ½ ripe avocado, peeled, stoned & cubed
- 75g/3oz strawberries, sliced
- ½ tsp paprika
- 1 shallot, finely chopped
- 2 tsp lime juice
- 1 tbsp freshly chopped coriander
- 125g/4oz watercress or rocket leaves
- Salt & pepper to taste

Method

1 Combine the cubed avocado, strawberries, paprika, shallots, lime & coriander together. Allow to sit for a few minutes to let the flavour infuse.

2 Pile onto a bed of watercress or rocket leaves, season & serve.

CHEFS NOTE

Stone the avocados by cutting in half (you'll need to work around the centre stone). When halved, dig the point of the knife into the stone to lever it out, then use a large spoon to scoop each half of the avocado out in one piece.

SCRAMBLED QUINOA OMELETTE

470 calories per serving

Ingredients

- 2 tsp olive oil
- ¼ red onion, sliced
- 1 yellow or orange pepper, deseeded & sliced
- ½ tsp each turmeric & paprika
- 50g/2oz cooked quinoa (cooked weight)
- 2 large free-range eggs
- Salt & pepper to taste
- 1 tbsp chopped flat leaf parsley

Method

1 Gently heat the olive oil in a frying pan and sauté the onions and pepper for a few minutes until softened.

2 Add the dried spices to the pan and stir. Cook for a minute or two longer before adding the eggs and quinoa to the pan.

3 Increase the heat, add seasoning and cook until the eggs are scrambled. Check the seasoning & serve immediately. Garnish with chopped parsley.

CHEFS NOTE
You could also serve this as a lunchtime meal with a crunchy green salad.

PARMESAN & ROASTED PEPPER FRITTATA

362 calories per serving

Ingredients

- 1 tsp olive oil
- 2 shallots, chopped
- 250g/9oz roasted peppers, drained & chopped
- 3 large free-range eggs
- 1 tbsp grated Parmesan cheese
- 2 sundried tomatoes, finely chopped
- 2 tbsp freshly chopped flat leaf parsley
- Salt & pepper to taste

Method

1 Heat the oil in a frying pan and gently sauté the shallots and peppers for a few minutes until softened. Add the peppers and continue to cook for 2-3 minutes longer.

2 Break the eggs into a bowl and combine with the Parmesan cheese. Tip the sautéed onions and peppers into the bowl along with the sundried tomatoes. Mix well and return the egg mixture to the pan, tilting to ensure the mixture covers the base evenly.

3 Cover the pan, reduce the heat and leave to cook for a few minutes. Flip the frittata over and cook the other side until the eggs set and the vegetables are tender.

4 Cut into wedges and serve with chopped parsley sprinkled over the top.

CHEFS NOTE
To keep things really simple use jars of precooked roasted peppers for this recipe.

POACHED EGG & MUSHROOM TOWER

375 calories per serving

Ingredients

- 1 tbsp soft cheese
- 2 tsp freshly chopped chives
- ½ garlic cloves, crushed
- 1 large flat mushroom

- 1 large free-range egg
- ½ avocado, stoned and sliced
- 1 handful rocket leaves
- Salt & pepper to taste

Method

1 Preheat the oven grill.

2 Mix the soft cheese, chives & garlic together and spread evenly on the underside of the mushroom. Season well and place, underside up, under the grill for 5-7 minutes or until the mushroom is cooked through.

3 Meanwhile fill a frying pan with boiling water and break the egg into the gently simmering pan to poach while the mushroom cooks.

4 Put the mushroom on the plate. Arrange the rocket over the top. Add the poached egg and pile the avocado slices on top.

CHEFS NOTE
Serve seasoned with plenty of black pepper over the top.

THE *Skinny*
BLOOD SUGAR
Diet
RECIPE BOOK

LUNCH

MEXICAN BEAN SOUP

280 calories per serving

Ingredients

- 2 tsp olive oil
- ½ garlic clove, crushed
- ¼ onion, sliced
- 120ml/½ cup vegetable stock
- 120ml/½ cup tomato passala/sieved tomatoes
- 50g/2oz vine ripened tomatoes, chopped
- 100g/3½oz tinned black-eyed beans, drained
- 2 tsp lime juice
- 1 tbsp freshly chopped coriander/cilantro
- Salt & pepper to taste

Method

1 Gently sauté the onion and garlic in the olive oil for a few minutes. Add all the ingredients, except the chopped coriander, to the pan.

2 Bring to the boil, cover and leave to simmer for 10-15 minutes or until everything is tender.

3 Blend to your preferred consistency, season and serve with coriander sprinkled over the top.

CHEFS NOTE
Use whichever beans you prefer for this filling soup.

MED SALAD SOUP

289
calories per serving

Ingredients

- 2 tsp olive oil
- 2 shallots, sliced
- 75g/3oz courgettes/zucchini, chopped
- 125g/4oz peas
- 50g/2oz spinach
- 1 celery stalk, chopped

- ¼ fennel bulb chopped
- 1 baby gem lettuce, shredded
- 250ml/1 cup vegetable stock
- 120ml/½ cup milk
- Salt & pepper to taste

Method

1 Heat a pan and gently sauté the shallots and courgettes in the olive oil for a few minutes. Add all the other ingredients, except the shredded lettuce and milk, to the pan.

2 Bring to the boil, cover and leave to gently simmer for 8-10 minutes or until everything is tender.

3 Blend to your preferred consistency stir through the milk and add the shredded lettuce. Stir through, season and serve immediately.

CHEFS NOTE

Adding fresh lettuce after cooking gives a lovely crunch to this unusual Mediterranean soup. You could add some finely chopped radishes too.

SEAFOOD COCKTAIL SALAD

389 calories per serving

Ingredients

- 1 tbsp mayonnaise
- 1 dash Tabasco sauce
- ½ tsp lemon juice
- 1 tsp freshly chopped chives
- 100g/3 ½ oz cooked & peeled prawns
- 100g/3 ½ oz cooked crabmeat
- 1 baby gem lettuce, shredded
- ½ ripe avocado, peeled, stoned & diced
- ¼ cucumber, diced
- Salt & pepper to taste

Method

1 Mix together the mayonnaise, Tabasco sauce, lemon juice, chives, prawns and crabmeat until everything is really well combined.

2 In a separate bowl gently combine the shredded lettuce, avocado & cucumber to make a salad.

3 Pile the dressed prawns and crabmeat on top and serve.

CHEFS NOTE
Sprinkle with a little paprika and serve with lemon wedges.

TUNA BEAN SALAD

520 calories per serving

Ingredients

- ½ cucumber, finely sliced into match-sticks
- ½ tsp honey
- 2 tsp rice wine vinegar
- Pinch dried chilli flakes
- 200g/7oz tinned borlotti beans, drained & rinsed
- 75g/3oz cherry tomatoes, halved
- 125g/5oz tinned tuna, drained
- ½ avocado, cubed
- 25g/5oz rocket
- ½ red onion, finely chopped
- Salt & pepper to taste

Method

1 Place the cucumber in a frying pan and gently warm over a low heat. Add the rice wine vinegar, honey & chilli flakes. Simmer for a few minutes and set aside to cool.

2 Meanwhile mix together the red onion, beans, tomatoes & tuna in a large bowl. Add the cooled cucumber, toss with the avocado and rocket and serve.

CHEFS NOTE
Use any kind of beans you prefer.

NUTTY SPROUT SALAD

215
calories per serving

Ingredients

- 150g/5oz prepared Brussels sprouts
- 2 tsp butter
- 3 shallots, sliced
- 1 tbsp slivered almonds
- A drizzle of extra virgin olive oil
- Salt & pepper to taste

Method

1 Slice the sprouts really thinly so they fall into shreds.

2 Heat the butter in a frying pan and gently sauté the shallots and almonds for a few minutes until the shallots are soft and golden.

3 Meanwhile plunge the shredded sprouts into salted boiling water for 2 minutes. Drain and rinse through with cold water. Add to the onion pan and toss until piping hot and cooked through.

4 Season with plenty of salt & freshly ground pepper and a drizzle of olive oil.

CHEFS NOTE
It is thought almonds can reduce the rise in blood sugar and insulin levels after meals.

FRESH ASPARAGUS & WATERCRESS SOUP

180 calories per serving

Ingredients

- 2 tsp olive oil
- ½ garlic clove, crushed
- 2 shallots, sliced
- 100g/3½oz asparagus tips
- 370ml/1½cups vegetable stock/broth
- 50g/2oz watercress
- Salt & pepper to taste

Method

1 Heat the oil and gently sauté the garlic, shallots and asparagus for a few minutes until softened.

2 Add all the ingredients to a saucepan. Bring to the boil and simmer for 3 minutes.

3 Roughly blend the soup with just a couple of pulses in the food processor. Check the seasoning and serve immediately.

CHEFS NOTE
A swirl of cream little cream makes a good addition to this subtle soup.

RYE & PARMESAN CRUSTED SALMON

440
calories per serving

Ingredients

- 50g/2oz bulgur wheat
- 1 boneless, skinless salmon fillet weighing 150g/5oz
- 2 tsp grated Parmesan cheese
- 1 tbsp fresh rye breadcrumbs
- ½ garlic clove, crushed
- 200g/7oz tenderstem broccoli
- Lemon wedges to serve
- Salt & pepper to taste

Method

1 Cook the bulgur wheat in salted boiling water for 15 minutes or until tender.

2 Meanwhile season the salmon fillet. Mix the Parmesan cheese, breadcrumbs & garlic together and coat the top of the salmon fillets with the breadcrumb mixture.

3 Place the salmon under a preheated grill and cook for 10-13 minutes or until the salmon fillets are cooked through.

4 Whilst the salmon is cooking plunge the broccoli into salted boiling water and cook for a 2-3 minutes or until tender.

5 Drain any excess liquid from the bulgur wheat and fluff with a fork. Drain the broccoli and serve with the salmon fillet, bulgur wheat and lemon wedges.

CHEFS NOTE
To make fresh breadcrumbs place a slice of rye bread in the food processor and pulse for a few seconds.

SIMPLE BROCCOLI & CAULIFLOWER SOUP

168 calories per serving

Ingredients

- 75g/3oz cauliflower florets, chopped
- 75g/3oz broccoli florets, chopped
- 100g/3½oz tinned cooked lentils
- 1 shallot, chopped
- 1 tbsp chopped flat leaf parsley
- 250ml/1 cups vegetable stock/broth
- 120ml/½ cup milk
- Salt & pepper to taste

Method

1 Add all the ingredients, except the milk, to the saucepan.

2 Bring to the boil and leave to gently simmer for 8-10 minutes or until the vegetables are tender.

3 Blend to a smooth consistency, add the milk, and heat through for a minute or two. Check the seasoning and serve with freshly chopped parsley sprinkled over the top.

CHEFS NOTE
Cooked lentils are widely available and are a great time saver.

SPICED MACKEREL FILLET

460 calories per serving

Ingredients

- 1 fresh, boned headless mackerel weighing 150g/5oz
- 1 tsp curry powder
- 1 tsp olive oil
- 1 tbsp horseradish sauce
- 1 tsp lemon juice
- 1 tsp chopped capers
- 100g/3½oz spinach
- Salt & pepper to taste

Method

1 Butterfly the mackerel to open into one large flat fillet. Season and rub with the curry powder.

2 Heat the olive oil in a pan and fry the mackerel for 3 minutes each side.

3 Meanwhile combine together the horseradish sauce, lemon juice & capers to make a dressing.

4 When the fish is cooked, wrap in foil and put to one side to keep warm. Add the spinach to the empty pan and cook for a few minutes. Stir the dressing through the wilted spinach and serve with the cooked mackerel fillets.

CHEFS NOTE
Some shop-bought horseradish can be high in salt so make sure you check the ingredients.

COD & CHUNKY SALSA

430 calories per serving

Ingredients

- 1 tsp lime juice
- 1 tsp white wine vinegar
- 6 cherry tomatoes, diced
- 1 spring onions, finely chopped
- ½ avocado, peeled & stoned
- 1 garlic clove, crushed
- 2 tsp olive oil
- 75g/3oz asparagus spears
- 1 boneless, skinless cod fillets weighing 150g/5oz
- 50g/2oz watercress
- Salt & pepper to taste

Method

1 Combine together the lime juice, vinegar, cherry tomatoes, spring onions and avocado to create a chunky salsa.

2 Mix together the garlic & olive oil and brush onto the cod fillet & asparagus spears.

3 Place the fish and asparagus under a preheated grill and cook for 6-9 minutes or until the cod is cooked through and the asparagus spears are tender

4 Season and serve the cooked cod with the salsa over the top and the watercress on the side of the plate.

CHEFS NOTE
Chopped coriander sprinkled over the salsa makes a good addition.

BALSAMIC TUNA & ZUCCHINI

370 calories per serving

Ingredients

- 2 medium courgettes/zucchinis, diced
- ½ red onion, finely chopped
- 3 tsp olive oil
- 1 fresh tuna steaks, weighing 150g/5oz
- 1 tbsp balsamic vinegar
- 75g/3oz rocket & watercress leaves
- Salt & pepper to taste

Method

1 Gently sauté the courgettes and red onion in 2 teaspoons of the olive oil for a few minutes until softened.

2 Season the tuna. Put a frying pan on a high heat with the rest of the olive oil and balsamic vinegar.

3 Place the tuna in the pan and cook for 2 minutes each side. Remove the tuna from the pan and serve with the watercress and courgette side dish.

CHEFS NOTE
Two minutes of cooking each side should leave the tuna rare in the centre. Reduce or increase cooking time depending on your preference.

FETA, PEPPERS & FILLET

SERVES 1

555
calories per
serving

Ingredients

- 150g/5oz filet steak
- 1 tbsp olive oil
- ½ onion, sliced
- ½ garlic clove, crushed
- 1 red or yellow pepper, deseeded & sliced

- ½ tsp paprika
- 100g/3½oz cherry tomatoes
- 1 baby gem lettuce
- 50g/2oz feta cheese, crumbled
- Salt & pepper to taste

Method

1 Lightly brush the steak with a little of the olive oil. Season and put a frying pan on a high heat.

2 In another pan gently sauté the peppers, paprika, onions & garlic in the rest of the olive oil for 5-7 minutes or until tender.

3 Place the steak in the smoking hot dry pan and cook for 2 minutes each side, or to your liking. Leave to rest for 3 minutes and then finely slice.

4 Halve the tomatoes & shred the lettuce. Place in a bowl, add the sliced peppers, crumble the feta cheese, combine well and then tip into a shallow bowl.

5 Place the sliced steak on top. Season and serve.

CHEFS NOTE
Fillet steak can be expensive so feel free to use whichever cut is within your budget.

WILD RICE & CHICKEN STIR-FRY

620 calories per serving

Ingredients

- 125g/4oz skinless chicken breast, sliced
- 100g/3½oz tenderstem broccoli
- 75g/3oz wild rice
- 2 tsp olive oil
- 1 garlic clove, crushed
- ½ onion, chopped
- 2 tsp soy sauce
- 60ml/ ¼ cup chicken stock/broth
- 1 tsp fish sauce
- 200g/7oz spinach leaves, chopped
- 1 fresh lime wedge
- 1 tbsp cashew nuts, chopped
- Salt & pepper to taste

Method

1 Season the chicken and roughly chop the broccoli.

2 Place the wild rice in salted boiling water and cook for 40-50 minutes or until tender.

3 Meanwhile heat the olive oil in a frying pan and gently sauté the garlic and onions for a few minutes.

4 Add the chicken & chopped broccoli to the pan along with the soy sauce, chicken stock & fish sauce. Stir-fry for 8-10 minutes until the chicken is cooked through.

5 Add the drained rice to the pan along with the spinach.

6 Combine for a minute or two, pile into a bowl with the nuts sprinkled over the top and the lime edge on the side. Check the seasoning and serve.

CHEFS NOTE
Thanks to the fibre it contains, wild rice doesn't cause the same blood sugar spike as white rice.

SUNDRIED TOMATO & CHICKEN SALAD

590 calories per serving

Ingredients

- 150g/5oz skinless chicken breast
- 75g/3oz cherry tomatoes
- 3 sundried tomatoes, finely chopped
- 25g/1oz Dolcelatte cheese
- ½ ripe avocado, peeled & stoned
- 2 tsp extra virgin olive oil

- 2 tsp cider vinegar
- 1 tbsp crème fraiche
- ½ tsp paprika
- 75g/3oz watercress
- Salt & pepper to taste

Method

1 Season the chicken fillet and place under a preheated grill for 15-20 minutes or until cooked through. Slice into strips and put to one side to cool.

2 Halve the cherry tomatoes and crumble the Dolcelatte cheese.

3 Combine together the olive oil, vinegar, crème fraiche & paprika to make a dressing.

4 Toss the dressing, tomatoes, sundried tomatoes, cheese & avocados together in a large bowl and serve on a bed of watercress with the chicken slices on top.

CHEFS NOTE
Feta cheese also works well in this recipe.

CREAMY DRESSED SALMON & CABBAGE

380 calories per serving

Ingredients

- 150g/5oz skinless salmon fillets
- ½ savoy cabbage, shredded
- 1 tbsp olive oil
- 1 garlic clove, crushed
- 1 tbsp freshly chopped chives

- 1 tbsp crème fraiche
- 2 tsp horseradish sauce
- 2 tsp lemon juice
- Salt & pepper to taste

Method

1 Season the salmon fillet and place under a preheated grill for 10-12 minutes or until cooked through. Flake and put to one side to cool.

2 Steam the cabbage for 8-10 minutes or until the cabbage is tender. Meanwhile heat the oil and garlic in a saucepan and gently sauté for a minute or two. Add the cooked cabbage, stir well and cook for a minute or two longer.

3 Gently combine together the chives, crème fraiche, horseradish sauce, lemon juice & cooled flaked salmon.

4 Arrange the dressed salmon and sautéed cabbage in a shallow bowl, season & serve.

CHEFS NOTE
Feel free to use precooked salmon fillets if you are short of time.

QUINOA CITRUS CHICKEN

550
calories per serving

Ingredients

- 50g/2oz quinoa
- 1 tbsp sultanas, chopped
- 125g/4oz skinless chicken breast
- 1 shallot, chopped
- 1 garlic clove, crushed
- 2 tsp lemon juice
- 1 tbsp olive oil
- Lemon wedges to serve
- 1 tbsp freshly chopped coriander/cilantro
- Salt & pepper to taste

Method

1 Cook the quinoa in the boiling vegetable stock or water for 15-20 minutes or until tender. Add the sultanas for the last few 2 minutes of cooking. Drain the quinoa and put to one side.

2 Meanwhile season the chicken breast meat. Grill for 15-20 mins or until cooked through and leave to cool before roughly chopping.

3 Gently sauté the chopped shallot, garlic, & lemon juice in the olive oil for a few minutes and add the chicken.

4 Fluff the quinoa with a fork and pile into the shallot pan. Mix well and serve with fresh lemon wedges on the side and chopped coriander sprinkled over the top.

CHEFS NOTE
Mint or flat leaf parsley is also a good addition to this dish if you want to put a different twist on things.

COURGETTE SPAGHETTI, TOMATOES & OLIVES

230 calories per serving

Ingredients

- 1 large courgette/zucchini
- 125g/4oz ripe cherry tomatoes
- 1 tbsp balsamic vinegar
- 8 pitted black olives, halved
- 1 tbsp olive oil
- 1 garlic clove, crushed
- ½ onion, sliced
- 1 tbsp freshly chopped basil
- Salt & pepper to taste

Method

1 First spiralize the courgette into thin spaghetti noodles.

2 Dice the ripe tomatoes and place in a bowl with the balsamic vinegar and some seasoning.

3 Heat the olive oil in a high-sided frying pan and gently sauté the garlic, onions, tomatoes and olives for a few minutes.

4 Add the courgette spaghetti and increase the heat. Stir fry for 2-3 minutes. Toss well, sprinkle with freshly chopped basil, season & serve.

CHEFS NOTE
You will need a Spiralizer for this dish if you don't have one pre-prepared shredded vegetables are now available in most supermarkets.

SERVES 1

PARSLEY & PARMESAN SPIRALS

190 calories per serving

Ingredients

- 1 large courgette/zucchini
- 1 tbsp extra virgin olive oil
- 1 garlic clove, crushed
- 2 shallots, sliced
- 1 tsp lemon juice
- 2 tbsp freshly chopped flat leaf parsley
- 1 tbsp grated Parmesan cheese
- Salt & pepper to taste

Method

1 First spiralize the courgette into thick spirals.

2 Heat the olive oil in a high-sided frying pan and gently sauté the garlic and shallots for a few minutes. Add the courgette spirals and increase the heat. Stir fry for 2-3 minutes.

3 Remove from the heat. Add the lemon juice, parsley and Parmesan. Toss well, season & serve.

CHEFS NOTE
You will need a Spiralizer for this dish if you don't have one pre-prepared shredded vegetables are now available in most supermarkets.

41

TENDER BROCCOLI WITH ANCHOVY DRESSING

255 calories per serving

Ingredients

- 4 tinned anchovy fillets
- 200g/7oz tenderstem broccoli
- 1 tbsp olive oil
- 1 garlic clove, crushed
- ½ onion, finely sliced
- ½ red chilli, deseeded & finely chopped
- Salt & pepper to taste

Method

1 Drain the anchovy fillets and put to one side.

2 Plunge the broccoli into a pan of salted boiling water and cook for 2 minutes. Drain and put to one side.

3 Heat the olive oil in a frying pan and gently sauté the garlic, onion, chilli, and anchovy fillets and cook for a few minutes until anchovies begin to break up.

4 Add the broccoli to the pan and increase the heat. Toss until well combined.

5 Check the seasoning and serve.

CHEFS NOTE
Tenderstem broccoli is great for making quick lunches and suppers. Use crushed chillies if you don't have fresh chillies to hand.

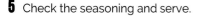

BAKED MACKEREL & OLIVES

575 calories per serving

Ingredients

- 1 tbsp olive oil
- ¼ onion, sliced
- ½ garlic clove, crushed
- 200g/7oz ripe plum tomatoes, roughly chopped
- 120ml/½ cup tomato passata/sieved tomatoes
- 10 pitted black olives, halved
- 2 tsp lemon juice
- Pinch of crushed chilli flakes
- 200g/7oz skinless, boneless mackerel fillets
- 1 tbsp freshly chopped basil
- Salt & pepper to taste

Method

1 Preheat the oven to 200C/400F/Gas Mark 6.

2 Gently sauté the onion and garlic in the olive oil for a few minutes until softened. Add the roughly chopped tomatoes & passata and leave to gently simmer for 10 minutes stirring occasionally. Add the olives, lemon juice & chilli flakes and combine well to make a rich tomato sauce.

3 Place the fish fillets in an ovenproof dish and pour over the tomato sauce. Season well and place in the oven. Cook for 20-30 minutes or until the fish is cooked through and piping hot. Sprinkle with chopped basil, season and serve.

CHEFS NOTE
Serve with a crisp green salad or steamed greens.

CHICKPEA PRAWN BOWL

420 calories per serving

Ingredients

- 1 tbsp olive oil
- ½ onion, sliced
- 1 garlic cloves, crushed
- ½ red chilli, deseeded & finely chopped
- 100g/3½oz ripe plum tomatoes, roughly chopped
- 200g/7oz tinned chickpeas, drained
- 150g/5oz peeled raw king prawns
- 2 tsp lemon juice
- 1 tbsp freshly chopped parsley
- Lemon wedges to serve
- Salt & pepper to taste

Method

1 Heat the olive in a pan and gently sauté the onion, garlic & chilli for a few minutes until softened.

2 Add the roughly chopped tomatoes & chickpeas and leave to gently simmer for 15 minutes stirring occasionally.

3 Add the prawns & lemon juice and combine well. Cover and simmer for a further 10 minutes or until the prawns are pink and cooked through.

4 Sprinkle with chopped basil and serve with lemon wedges.

CHEFS NOTE
Try serving with leafy greens or wild rice.

CITRUS HERB BULGUR SALAD

260 calories per serving

Ingredients

- 50g/2oz bulgur wheat
- 1 tbsp pine nuts
- ½ onion, chopped
- ½ garlic clove, crushed
- 1 tbsp lime juice
- 1 tbsp olive oil
- 1 bunch spring onions/scallions, sliced lengthways
- Lime wedges to serve
- 2 tbsp freshly chopped mixed herbs
- 1 romaine lettuce, shredded
- Salt & pepper to taste

Method

1 Cook the bulgur wheat in salted boiling water for 15 minutes or until tender.

2 Place the pine nuts in a dry frying pan and lightly toast for a minute or two. Put to one side and use the same pan to gently sauté the chopped onions & garlic for a few minutes.

3 Add the lime juice, fluff the bulgar with a fork and pile into the onion pan along with the toasted pine nuts. Mix well, and serve over the shredded lettuce with fresh lime wedges on the side and the herbs & spring onions sprinkled over the top.

CHEFS NOTE
This simple dish is lovely served alone but is a great side to grilled tuna too.

SLOW ROASTED FETA TOMATOES

305 calories per serving

Ingredients

- 300g/10oz ripe plum tomatoes
- ½ tsp each dried thyme & oregano
- 1 tbsp olive oil
- 2 tbsp freshly chopped parsley
- 50g/2oz feta cheese
- Salt & pepper to taste

Method

1 Preheat the oven to its absolutely lowest heat setting.

2 Place all the ingredients, except the parsley & feta cheese, in a bowl and mix well. Tip the tomatoes onto a grilling rack with a tray underneath to catch the juices.

3 Place in the preheated oven and leave to cook for approx. 5-6 hours.

4 Sprinkle with chopped parsley & crumbled feta cheese and serve.

CHEFS NOTE
You can of course speed this up by increasing the heat of the oven and cooking for a shorter time.

SIMPLE CAPONATA

370 calories per serving

Ingredients

- 1 tbsp olive oil
- 1 aubergine/egg plant, cubed
- ¼ red onion, chopped
- 1 celery stalk, chopped
- ½ garlic clove, crushed
- 1 tbsp balsamic vinegar
- 1 tsp capers, chopped

- 75g/3oz ripe tomatoes, roughly chopped
- 5 black pitted olives, sliced
- 1 tsp sultanas, roughly chopped
- 1 tbsp freshly chopped parsley
- 50g/2oz feta cheese
- Salt & pepper to taste

Method

1 Gently sauté the prepared aubergine, onions, celery and garlic in the olive oil for a few minutes until softened.

2 Add the balsamic vinegar, capers, tomatoes, olives & sultanas. Stir, cover and continue to very gently cook for 20-25 minutes or until everything is cooked through and tender.

3 Sprinkle with chopped parsley and crumbled feta and serve.

CHEFS NOTE
You can also make this dish by slowly roasting in the oven with a splash of vegetable stock.

FRESH SARDINES

330
calories per
serving

Ingredients

- 2 fresh sardines each weighing 125g/4oz
- 1 garlic clove, crushed
- 2 tsp extra virgin olive oil
- 1 tsp lemon juice
- Large pinch of paprika
- 1 tbsp freshly chopped oregano
- Lemon wedges to serve
- Salt & pepper to taste

Method

1 Preheat the grill to a medium/high heat.

2 Ask your fishmonger to prepare the sardines by gutting, cleaning & boning them for you. Mix together the garlic, olive oil, lemon juice & paprika and brush onto either side of each fish.

3 Place the sardines under the grill and cook for 4-5 minutes each side or until the sardines are cooked through. Remove from the grill, season and serve with lemon wedges and oregano sprinkled over the top.

CHEFS NOTE
These lightly dressed sardines are also easy to cook on the barbeque.

THE *Skinny*
BLOOD SUGAR
Diet
RECIPE BOOK

DINNER

SERVES 1

SPICED CHICKEN & LO-CARB RICE

540
calories per serving

Ingredients

- 50g/2oz red onion, chopped
- 75g/3oz green beans
- 1 garlic clove, crushed
- 1 tbsp extra virgin olive oil
- 125g/4oz cherry tomatoes, chopped
- 1 tbsp sultanas
- 150g/5oz chicken breast, sliced
- 2 tsp medium curry powder
- 2 tbsp coconut cream
- 2 tbsp flat leaf parsley, chopped
- 200g/7oz cauliflower florets
- 1 tbsp chopped coriander/cilantro
- Salt & pepper to taste

Method

1 Get the onions, green beans, garlic, cherry tomatoes & sultanas gently cooking in a frying pan with the olive oil. Sauté for a few minutes and then add the chicken & curry powder (add a little more olive oil if needed).

2 Cook for a few minutes until the chicken is cooked thorough then stir through the coconut cream and parsley.

3 Meanwhile place the cauliflower florets in a food processor and pulse a few times until the cauliflower is the size of rice grains.

4 Place the 'rice' in a microwavable dish, cover and cook on full power for about 90 seconds minutes or until it's piping hot.

5 Tip the 'rice' into a shallow bowl. Serve the chicken and vegetables over the top sprinkled with chopped coriander.

CHEFS NOTE
Prawns or pork are also good in this simple spiced dish.

50

POMEGRANATE HERBED QUINOA

455 calories per serving

Ingredients

- 75g/3oz quinoa
- 3 tbsp pomegranate seeds
- 2 tsp lemon juice
- 1 tbsp extra virgin olive oil
- 1 tbsp fresh mint, chopped
- 2 tbsp flat leaf parsley, chopped
- 50g/2oz carrot, grated
- 50g/2oz celery, sliced
- 50g/2oz feta cheese, crumbled
- 1 tbsp balsamic vinegar
- Salt & pepper to taste

Method

1 Put the quinoa in a saucepan, cover and cook in boiling water for about 15 minutes or until it's tender. (Cook in vegetable stock if you wish, rather than water.)

2 Once the quinoa is ready, drain it and fluff with a fork. Combine with the pomegranate seeds, lemon juice, olive oil, mint and parsley. Pile the grated carrot and sliced celery on top.

3 Add the crumbled feta cheese and drizzle the balsamic vinegar over the cheese. Season and serve.

CHEFS NOTE
Add as much balsamic vinegar as you like to this crunchy quinoa salad.

VIETNAMESE PRAWNS

505 calories per serving

Ingredients

- 50g/2oz brown rice
- 1 tbsp extra virgin olive oil
- 50g/2oz red onion
- 50g/2oz green beans, chopped
- 2 garlic cloves, crushed
- 1 birds eye chilli, sliced (leave the seeds in)
- 2 tbsp lime juice
- 2 tbsp fish sauce
- ½ tsp brown sugar
- 125g/4oz cooked prawns, chopped
- 1 tbsp flat leaf parsley, chopped
- 50g/2oz spinach
- Salt & pepper to taste

Method

1 Cook the rice in salted boiling water until tender and drain.

2 Meanwhile heat up a frying pan with the olive oil and start sautéing the onions for a few minutes until softened

3 While the onions are cooking combine the garlic cloves, chilli, lime juice, fish sauce and brown sugar to make a spicy, sweet & sour dressing.

4 Tip the drained rice and prawns into the pan with the onions and warm for a few minutes until everything is piping hot. Add the spinach for the last 60 seconds until it is gently wilted.

5 Tip the prawns & rice into a shallow bowl, drizzle the dressing over the top and sprinkle with parsley.

CHEFS NOTE

Balance the chilli, lime and sugar to suit your own taste in the fiery Vietnamese dressing.

COCONUT MILK EGG MOLEE

450 calories per serving

Ingredients

- 1 garlic clove, crushed
- 1 onion, chopped
- 75g/3oz peas
- 2 tsp olive oil
- 1 tbsp tomato puree
- 200g/7oz tinned chopped tomatoes
- ½ tsp each turmeric, garam masala & ground coriander/cilantro
- 250ml/1 cup tinned coconut milk
- 3 large free-range hard-boiled eggs
- 1 tbsp freshly chopped coriander/cilantro
- Salt & pepper to taste

Method

1 Gently sauté the garlic, onions & peas in the olive oil for a few minutes until softened.

2 Stir through the tomato puree, tinned chopped tomatoes, dried spices & coconut milk until combined. Cut the eggs in half and place yolk side up, in the coconut milk. Gently cook until warmed through.

3 When everything is piping hot, season and serve with chopped coriander over the top.

CHEFS NOTE

Try serving this with cauliflower 'rice'. To do this pulse cauliflower florets in a food processor and microwave for about 90 seconds or until piping hot.

EDAMAME CHICKEN

410
calories per serving

Ingredients

- 2 tsp olive oil
- ½ red onion, sliced
- ½ garlic clove, crushed
- 1 celery stalk, chopped
- 150g/5oz skinless chicken breasts, thickly sliced

- 1 tbsp fresh chopped marjoram
- 60ml/¼ cup chicken stock/broth
- 75g/3oz fresh edamame beans
- 125g/4oz spinach leaves
- Salt & pepper to taste

Method

1 In a saucepan gently sauté the onion, celery and garlic in the olive oil for a few minutes until softened.

2 Add the chicken, marjoram & stock and leave to gently simmer for 8-10 minutes or until the chicken is cooked through and the stock has reduced.

3 Add the edamame and cook for a minute or two.

4 Add the spinach and stir for a minute or two until wilted. Season and serve.

CHEFS NOTE
Edamame are delicious Asian soya beans.

FENNEL, CHICKEN & BEANS

485 calories per serving

Ingredients

- 2 tsp olive oil
- ¼ onion, sliced
- ½ fennel bulb, finely sliced
- 1 garlic cloves, crushed
- 60ml/¼ cup chicken stock/broth
- 200g/7oz tinned flageolet beans, drained
- 150g/5oz skinless chicken breasts, thickly sliced
- 1 tbsp freshly chopped basil
- 1 tsp Parmesan shavings
- Salt & pepper to taste

Method

1 Gently sauté the onion, fennel and garlic in the olive oil for a few minutes until softened.

2 Add the beans, chicken & stock and leave to gently simmer for 10-15 minutes or until the chicken is cooked through and the stock has reduced.

3 Sprinkle with chopped basil and Parmesan shaving. Season and serve.

CHEFS NOTE
Parmesan and fennel are a classic Italian combination.

SALMON & FENNEL

370
calories per serving

Ingredients

- 2 tsp olive oil
- ½ onion, sliced
- ¼ fennel bulb, finely sliced
- 1 garlic cloves, crushed
- 1 celery stalks, chopped
- 200g/7oz ripe plum tomatoes, roughly chopped
- 60ml/¼ cup vegetable or chicken stock/ broth
- 150g/5oz skinless, boneless salmon fillet
- Lemon wedges to serve
- 1 tbsp freshly chopped flat leaf parsley
- Salt & pepper to taste

Method

1 In a shallow saucepan gently sauté the onion, fennel, garlic & celery in the olive oil for a few minutes until softened.

2 Add the roughly chopped tomatoes & stock and leave to gently simmer for 10 minutes stirring occasionally.

3 Add the fish fillet and gently combine well. Cover and simmer for a further 8-10 minutes or until the fish is cooked through and the sauce has reduced.

4 Season well and serve with lemon wedges and parsley sprinkled over the top.

CHEFS NOTE
To keep the salmon fillet whole you could grill it separately and serve over the tomato and fennel sauce when it's ready.

PRAWN & PARSLEY QUINOA

295 calories per serving

Ingredients

- 50g/2oz quinoa
- 1 tsp olive oil
- 1 garlic clove, crushed
- 200g/7oz raw, shelled king prawns
- 1 tbsp lemon juice
- 2 tbsp freshly chopped flat leaf parsley
- 1 romaine lettuce shredded
- Salt & pepper to taste

Method

1 Put the quinoa in a saucepan, cover and cook in boiling water for about 15 minutes or until it is tender. (Cook in vegetable stock if you wish rather than water.)

2 Meanwhile heat the olive oil and gently sauté the garlic, prawns & lemon juice whilst the quinoa cooks.

3 When the prawns are cooked through and the quinoa is tender, drain any excess liquid from the quinoa and add to the frying pan with the prawns.

4 Toss well. Arrange the shredded lettuce in a shallow bowl and pile the prawns and quinoa on top. Sprinkle with chopped parsley and serve.

CHEFS NOTE
Prawns, lemon and garlic are a match made in heaven. Add more garlic if you prefer a stronger taste.

SUNDRIED TOMATO & CAPER GRAINS

260 calories per serving

Ingredients

- 75g/3oz quinoa
- 200g/7oz ripe cherry tomatoes
- 1 tbsp capers
- 1 tbsp sultanas
- 2 tsp olive oil

- ½ garlic clove, crushed
- 3 sundried tomatoes (from a jar)
- 1 tbsp freshly chopped basil
- Salt & pepper to taste

Method

1 Put the quinoa in a saucepan, cover and cook in boiling water for about 15 minutes or until it's tender. (Cook in vegetable stock if you wish rather than water.)

2 Half the cherry tomatoes and roughly chop the capers, sultanas and sundried tomatoes.

3 Heat the olive oil and gently sauté the garlic, cherry tomatoes, capers, sultanas and sundried tomatoes whilst the quinoa cooks. When the quinoa grains are tender drain any excess water and add to the frying pan.

4 Toss well and serve with chopped basil on top.

CHEFS NOTE

This is good served on a bed of rocket and spinach.

ZUCCHINI & BLACK OLIVE BULGUR WHEAT

345 calories per serving

Ingredients

- 75g/3oz bulgur wheat
- 100g/3½oz baby courgettes/zucchini
- 8 pitted black olives, sliced
- ½ onion, chopped
- 1 garlic clove, crushed
- 1 tbsp lemon juice
- 2 tsp olive oil
- Lemon wedges to serve
- 1 tbsp freshly chopped mint
- Salt & pepper to taste

Method

1 Cook the bulgur wheat in boiling water for 15 minutes or until tender. (Cook in vegetable stock if you wish rather than water.)

2 Use a vegetable peeler to cut the courgettes into ribbons.

3 Gently sauté the sliced olives, chopped onions, garlic, lemon juice and courgette ribbons in the olive oil for a few minutes.

4 When the bulgur wheat is ready drain off any excess water. Fluff the bulgur wheat with a fork and pile into the onion and courgette pan. Mix well, divide onto plates and serve with fresh lemon wedges on the side and chopped mint sprinkled over the top.

CHEFS NOTE
You could use chopped basil or coriander in place of mint if you like.

FRESH MINT FISH

340
calories per
serving

Ingredients

- 150g/5oz skinless, boneless fish fillets
- ½ garlic clove, crushed
- 2 tsp extra virgin olive oil
- 2 tsp lemon juice
- 1 tbsp freshly chopped mint
- 2 large ripe beef tomatoes, thickly sliced
- ½ red onion finely sliced into rounds
- 50g/2oz mozzarella cheese, sliced
- Salt & pepper to taste

Method

1 Mix together the garlic, olive oil & lemon juice and brush on either side of the fish fillet.

2 Place the fish under the grill and cook for 2-3 minutes each side or until the fillet is cooked through.

3 Meanwhile arrange the sliced tomatoes, red onion and mozzarella on the plate.

4 Sit the cooked fish to the side of the salon and sprinkle the mint all over.

CHEFS NOTE
Use whichever fish you prefer. Oily is best.

PRAWN & PINEAPPLE SKEWERS

320 calories per serving

Ingredients

- ½ garlic clove, crushed
- 1 tbsp extra virgin olive oil
- 2 tsp lime juice
- 150g/5oz large king prawns
- 75g/3oz pineapple chunks
- 1 red pepper, cut into chunks
- Salt & pepper to taste
- Metal skewers

Method

1 Preheat the grill to a medium/high heat.

2 Mix together the garlic, olive oil & lime juice in a bowl. Season the prawns, peppers and pineapple pieces and add to the bowl.

3 Combine well and skewer each piece in turn to make two large kebabs. Place under the grill and cook for 4-5 minutes each side or until the prawns are pink and cooked through.

4 Remove from the grill, season and serve.

CHEFS NOTE
These skewers are great served with wild rice and a dollop of Greek yoghurt.

VEGETABLE WHOLEWHEAT SALAD

660 calories per serving

Ingredients

- 50g/2oz giant whole wheat couscous
- 1 tbsp olive oil
- ½ garlic clove, crushed
- 1 red pepper, sliced
- ½ aubergine/egg plant, cubed
- ½ red onion, chopped
- 75g/3oz cherry tomatoes, halved
- 50g/2oz spinach leaves
- 50g/2oz feta cheese
- Salt & pepper to taste

Method

1 Prepare the couscous according to the instructions on the packet.

2 Mix the olive oil, garlic, peppers, aubergine, onions and tomatoes in a bowl. Add to a frying pan and gently sauté for 10 minutes or until all the vegetables are tender and cooked through.

3 Add the cooked rye grains to the pan and combine well. Pile everything on a plate on top of the spinach, crumble over the feta cheese. Season and serve.

CHEFS NOTE
Add some chopped sundried tomatoes for extra depth in flavour.

BROAD BEAN & OREGANO LENTILS

390 calories per serving

Ingredients

- 200g/7oz cooked tinned lentils
- 200g/7oz shelled fresh broad beans
- 2 tsp olive oil
- 3 anchovy fillets, drained
- ½ garlic clove, crushed
- 2 shallots, sliced

- 100g/3½oz ripe plum tomatoes, roughly chopped
- 1 tbsp freshly chopped oregano
- 50g/2oz rocket
- Salt & pepper to taste

Method

1 Place the broad beans in a pan of boiling water, cook for 2 minutes and drain.

2 Meanwhile heat the olive oil in a high-sided frying pan and gently sauté the anchovy fillets, garlic, onions, chopped tomatoes and oregano. Once cooked, leave to cool.

3 Drain the lentils and toss well with the cooled tomato mix.

4 Pile onto top of a bed or rocket and serve.

CHEFS NOTE
Try garnishing this with some extra fresh tomatoes, raw red onions and chopped basil.

SPICY MUSSELS

305 calories per serving

Ingredients

- 500g/1lb 2oz mussels
- 1 tbsp olive oil
- ½ garlic clove, crushed
- 1 shallot, sliced
- ½ red chilli, deseeded & finely chopped
- 200g/7oz tinned chopped tomatoes
- 60ml/¼ cup vegetable stock
- 1 tbsp freshly chopped basil
- Salt & pepper to taste

Method

1 Make sure the mussels are cleaned to get rid of any debris or seaweed. Place in a colander and rinse thoroughly under running water.

2 Heat the oil in a large lidded pan and gently sauté the garlic, shallots and chilli. After a few minutes increase the heat and add the chopped tomatoes and vegetable stock.

3 Place the mussels in the pan, cover with the lid and steam, for approximately 4-5 minutes, shaking the pan occasionally.

4 Tip the mussels and sauce into a shallow bowl. sprinkle with basil and serve.

CHEFS NOTE
Discard any mussels that remain shut after cooking. These should not be eaten.

MARJORAM GRILLED TUNA

295 calories per serving

Ingredients

- 1 fresh tuna steak weighing 150g/5oz
- 1 tbsp extra virgin olive oil
- 2 tsp lemon juice
- 1 tbsp freshly chopped marjoram
- 75g/3oz rocket & spinach leaves
- 75g/3oz vine ripened tomatoes, sliced
- 1 tbsp Parmesan shavings
- Lemon wedges to serve
- Salt & pepper to taste

Method

1 Preheat the grill to a medium/high heat.

2 Mix together the olive oil, lemon juice & marjoram and lightly brush on either side of the steak (reserving any remaining juice).

3 Place the tuna steak under the grill and cook for 2-3 minutes each side or until the tuna is cooked to your liking.

4 Remove from the grill, season and place on a plate with the green leaves and tomatoes. Drizzle any remaining juice over the top along with the Parmesan shavings. Serve with the lemon wedges.

CHEFS NOTE

Fresh tuna is best served rare in the centre, but feel free to adjust to your own taste.

GRILLED ASPARAGUS

220 calories per serving

Ingredients

- 125g/5oz asparagus spears
- 2 tsp olive oil
- Pinch dried chilli flakes
- 1 tsp balsamic vinegar
- 2 slices Parma ham
- Salt & pepper to taste

Method

1 Preheat the grill to a medium/high heat.

2 In a bowl mix together all the ingredients, except the ham, ensuring each asparagus spear is coated with oil.

3 Place under the grill and cook for 4-6 minutes each side or until cooked through.

4 Remove from the grill, season and serve immediately with the Parma ham laid over the top.

CHEFS NOTE
Feel free to replace Parma ham with some finely chopped sundried tomatoes.

HALLOUMI & BULGUR WHEAT

360 calories per serving

Ingredients

- 50g/2oz sliced halloumi
- ½ onion, chopped
- ½ garlic clove, crushed
- 1 red pepper, deseeded & finely chopped
- 2 tsp olive oil
- 50g/2oz bulgar wheat
- 1 tbsp freshly chopped flat leaf parsley
- Salt & pepper to taste

Method

1 Cook the bulgur wheat in salted boiling water for 15 minutes or until tender.

2 Meanwhile gently sauté the chopped onions, garlic & peppers in the olive oil until softened.

3 In a separate pan add the halloumi . You don't need to use any oil. Cook the first side of the halloumi for a minute or two. Flip and cook for a further minutes.

4 Drain the bulgur wheat and fluff with a fork. Combine in the pan with the peppers and onions.

5 Pile into a shallow bowl. Sit the halloumi on top, sprinkle with parsley and serve.

CHEFS NOTE
This is also good with quinoa or a combination of quinoa and bulgur wheat.

FRESH CHICKEN KEBABS

420 calories per serving

Ingredients

- ½ garlic clove, crushed
- 1 tbsp olive oil
- 2 tsp lime juice
- 150g/5oz skinless chicken breast, cubed
- 1 red pepper, deseeded & cut onto chunks
- 1 red onion, peeled and cut into chunks
- 8 button mushrooms
- 2 tbsp freshly chopped coriander/cilantro
- Salt & pepper to taste
- Metal skewers

Method

1 Preheat the grill to a medium/high heat.

2 Mix together the garlic, olive oil & lime juice in a bowl. Season the chicken and vegetables and add to the oil. Combine well and skewer each piece in turn to make 2 chicken and vegetable kebabs.

3 Place under the grill and cook for 6-8 minutes each side or until the chicken is cooked through and piping hot. Remove from the grill, season and serve with chopped coriander sprinkled over the top.

CHEFS NOTE
Substitute the coriander with any fresh herbs you prefer.

PESTO CHICKEN

460
calories per
serving

Ingredients

- 150g/5oz chicken breast
- ½ red onion, thickly sliced
- 2 tsp green pesto
- 50g/5oz French beans
- 50g/5oz ripe cherry tomatoes, halved
- 1 tsp dried oregano
- 1 tsp olive oil
- Salt & pepper to taste

Method

1 Preheat the oven to 200/400/gas Mark 5

2 Hold the chicken breast as if you were slicing through the centre of it. Stop slicing before you cut it in half completely (this will butterfly the breast). Open the chicken breast to expose the two inside parts. Spread the inside of each breast with the pesto and close the 'sandwich' back up so you are left with pesto through the centre of the chicken breast.

3 Place the chicken, onions, beans and tomatoes in a casserole dish. Season well, sprinkle with the dried oregano, brush with olive oil and cover with foil.

4 Place in the oven and leave to cook for 25-30 minutes or until the chicken is cooked through and the vegetables are tender. Remove from the oven and arrange the beans, tomatoes and onions as a bed onto which you serve each pesto chicken breast.

CHEFS NOTE

Add a splash of vegetable stock to the casserole dish if you want to keep the vegetables moist.

BALSAMIC TUNA STEAKS & COURGETTES

360 calories per serving

Ingredients

- 1 fresh tuna steaks, weighing 150g/5oz
- 1 tbsp olive oil
- 1 tbsp balsamic vinegar
- 75g/3oz baby courgettes/zucchini
- 1 garlic clove, crushed
- 1 tbsp freshly chopped chives
- 50g/2oz rocket leaves
- Salt & pepper to taste

Method

1 Preheat the grill to a medium/high heat.

2 Place the tuna on a plate. Mix together half of the olive oil & all the balsamic vinegar. Pour over the top of the steak to marinate for a few minutes. Turn the steak over and make sure both sides are brushed well with oil and vinegar.

3 Cut the courgettes in half lengthways and brush with the remaining tablespoon of olive oil and the crushed garlic.

4 Place the tuna steaks and courgettes under the grill and cook for 2-3 minutes each side or until the tuna is cooked to your liking and the courgettes are tender. Remove from the grill, place on top of the rocket leaves. Sprinkle with chives and serve.

CHEFS NOTE
Use any type of salad leaves you prefer with the tuna steak.

SPICY GARLIC PORK & MUSHROOMS

400 calories per serving

Ingredients

- 1 tsp olive oil
- 150g/5oz pork tenderloin, cubed
- 3 garlic cloves, peeled & finely sliced
- ½ onion, chopped
- 125g/4oz button mushrooms, sliced
- 2 tsp hot curry powder
- 1 tbsp tomato puree/paste
- 2 vine ripened tomatoes, roughly chopped
- 120ml/½ cup tomato passata/sieved tomatoes
- 60ml/¼ cup vegetable stock/broth
- 50g/2oz spinach leaves
- Salt & pepper to taste

Method

1 Season the pork and quickly brown for a couple of minutes in a frying pan with a little of the olive oil. Remove from the pan and put to one side.

2 Gently sauté the garlic, onions and mushrooms in the same pan with a little more oil for a few minutes until softened.

3 Add the rest of the ingredients, except the spinach, stir well and simmer for 15-20 minutes or until the pork is cooked through and tender. Serve on a bed of spinach leaves.

CHEFS NOTE
If you prefer your spinach wilted add to the pan 60 seconds before serving and combine with the pork.

GINGER BEEF & PINEAPPLE

590 calories per serving

Ingredients

- 125g/4oz good quality lean steak
- ½ red chilli, deseeded & finely chopped
- 2 tbsp rice wine vinegar
- Pinch of brown sugar
- 1 tbsp soy sauce
- 50g/2oz wild rice
- 1 tsp olive oil
- ½ onion, sliced
- 1 tbsp freshly grated ginger
- 75g/3oz tinned pineapple chunks, drained
- Salt & pepper to taste

Method

1 Trim any fat off the steak, season and thinly slice. Place in a bowl with the chopped chilli, vinegar, brown sugar & soy sauce. Combine well and leave to marinade for 15-20 minutes.

2 Cook the wild rice in salted boiling water until tender.

3 Meanwhile heat the olive oil and gently stir-fry the onions & ginger for a few minutes until softened.

4 Increase the heat and add the marinated steak & pineapples chunks. Stir-fry until the sauce thickens up and the dish is piping hot.

5 Serve with the drained wild rice.

CHEFS NOTE
Ginger is an excellent blood 'cleansing' spice.

LAMB KOFTA

410
calories per
serving

Ingredients

- 125g/4oz lean lamb mince
- ½ tsp each ground cumin & coriander
- 1 garlic clove, crushed
- 1 tsp olive oil
- 1 cereal pitta bread

- 1 baby gem lettuce, shredded
- 1 tbsp fat free Greek yoghurt
- 1 tsp mint sauce
- 2 kebab skewers
- Salt & pepper to taste

Method

1 Preheat the grill.

2 Place the lamb mince, cumin, coriander, garlic & salt in a food processor and pulse to combine. Scoop out the mixture and use your hands to form into 2 balls.

3 Roll the balls into oval shapes and thread lengthways onto the skewers. Spray with a brush with olive oil, place under a preheated medium grill and cook for 8-12 minutes or until cooked through.

4 Mix the yoghurt and mint sauce together.

5 Warm the pitta bread under the grill, take the koftas off the skewers and place in the pittas along with the shredded lettuce & mint yoghurt.

CHEFS NOTE
Cereal pitta bread is made using a combination cereals including Linseed, Sunflower Seeds, Chunky Oats, Quinoa and Rye.

THE *Skinny*
BLOOD SUGAR
Diet
RECIPE BOOK

DESSERT

SIMPLE BERRY MINT MOUSSE

278 calories per serving

Ingredients

- 225g/8oz strawberries
- 1 tsp stevia
- ½ tsp vanilla extract
- 2 tbsp coconut oil
- 2 tbsp coconut butter
- 1 tbsp lemon juice
- 2 fresh mint leaves, chopped

Method

1 Cut the green tops off the strawberries.

2 Very gently warm the coconut oil and butter together until combined. Place all the ingredients in a blender and whizz until smooth. Pour into a small bowl and chill for a couple of hours until firm.

CHEFS NOTE
Leave out the mint if you prefer.

ALMOND & CHOCOLATE COOKIES

55 calories per cookie

Ingredients

- 375g/13oz almond flour
- ½ tsp sea salt
- ¼ tsp baking soda
- 1 tsp each ground cinnamon & almonds
- 100g/3½oz cocoa nibs
- 2 tsp vanilla extract
- 60ml/¼ cup coconut oil

Method

1 Mix together the flour, salt, baking powder, cinnamon, ground almonds and coca nibs. In a separate bowl mix together the oil & vanilla and, when combined, mix the contents of each bowl together to make a ball of dough. Cover and leave to chill for about an hour.

2 Preheat the oven to 180C/350F/Gas Mark 5.

3 Roll out the dough onto a floured surface (use a little almond flour) until the dough is about 1cm/¼ inch thick. Use a small cookie cutter to make approx. 30 cookies (depending on the size of your cutter).

4 Place the cut cookies on baking parchment on a baking tray and cook in the preheated oven for 5-7 minutes or until they begin to gently brown. Take out of the oven and leave to cool on a rack.

CHEFS NOTE

This recipe makes far more cookies than one person would need in a single sitting but they store well.

MINI MERINGUES

65
calories per
meringue

Ingredients

- 5 large egg whites
- 1 tsp stevia
- ¼ tsp sea salt
- 125g/4oz unsweetened coconut flakes

Method

1 Use a mixer to whisk together the egg whites and stevia to form stiff peaks. Gently 'fold' in the salt and coconut flakes, using the minimum amount of folding to keep all the air in the egg white mixture. Cover and place in the refrigerator to chill for 30-40 minutes.

2 Preheat the oven to 180C/350F/Gas Mark 5.

3 Lay out a piece of baking parchment on an oven tray. Use a small ice cream scoop to make meringue mounds which you turn-out onto the baking parchment. (Make sure each scoop is packed tight by pressing down with the palm of your hand on the filling when it is in the scoop). Bake in a preheated oven for 9-12 minutes or until the meringues gently begin to brown.

CHEFS NOTE

This bite-size light dessert is delicious and super simple to make.

BITE-SIZE BROWNIE BALLS

145
calories per brownie

Ingredients

- 125g/4oz coconut flour
- 100g/3½oz cocoa nibs
- Pinch sea salt
- 1 tsp baking powder

- 1 tsp vanilla extract
- 2 tbsp coconut oil
- 1 tbsp water
- 2 tbsp almond butter, melted

Method

1 Preheat the oven to 180C/350F/Gas Mark 5.

2 Combine all the ingredients into a dough and form into 8-10 balls with your hands. Lay out on a piece of baking parchment on a baking tray and cook for 20-25 minutes or until cooked through.

CHEFS NOTE

Use extra flour or water/oil as needed if you find the dough is too wet or dry during preparation.

COCONUT FLOUR PANCAKES

280 calories per serving

Ingredients

- 2 eggs
- 2 tbsp coconut milk
- 1 tbsp coconut flour

- 2 tsp olive oil
- ½ tsp vanilla extract

Method

1 Place all the ingredients in a blender and whizz until smooth.

2 Heat a little coconut oil in a small frying pan on a high heat. Pour in half the batter and fry until golden underneath (about 1 min if the pan is hot enough), flip and fry for a minute longer.

CHEFS NOTE
These make a great breakfast too when paired with some Greek yoghurt and blueberries.

THE *Skinny* BLOOD SUGAR *Diet* RECIPE BOOK

SNACKS

EVERYDAY JUICE

140
calories per
serving

Ingredients

- 2 celery stalks
- 75g/3oz spinach
- 1 green apple
- 50g/2oz strawberries

- 1 tbsp lemon juice
- 1 tbsp flat leaf parsley
- Pinch of Matcha tea
- 3 tbsp water

Method

1 Rinse the celery, spinach, apple & strawberries. Core and peel the apple. Remove any thick stalks from the spinach. Chop the celery and strawberries.

2 Add everything to a blender. Twist on the blade and blend until smooth. Add some water if you want a thinner consistency.

CHEFS NOTE
This is a simple everyday juice packed with goodness.

MUHAMMARA DIP

245
calories per
serving

Ingredients

- 1 garlic clove
- 1 tsp paprika
- ½ tsp ground cumin
- 1 tbsp tomato puree/ paste
- 12 walnut halves
- 250g/9oz chargrilled peppers (from a jar)
- 2 tbsp olive oil
- 1 tbsp red wine vinegar
- Salt & pepper to taste

Method

1 Crush the garlic clove and roughly chop the walnuts.

2 Add all the ingredients to a food processor and pulse until smooth. Adjust the seasoning and serve.

CHEFS NOTE
Add more red wine vinegar and olive oil if you need to loosen the dip up a little.

TABASCO & AVOCADO DIP

210 calories per serving

Ingredients

- 2 tbsp lemon juice
- ½-1 tsp Tabasco sauce
- ½ tsp ground cumin
- 300g/11oz tinned chickpeas, drained
- 1 garlic clove, crushed
- 1 ripe avocado
- 2 tbsp olive oil
- Salt & pepper to taste

Method

1 Give the chickpeas a rinse in cold water.

2 Crush the garlic clove, remove the stone from the avocado and add all the ingredients to a food processor.

3 Pulse until smooth. Adjust the seasoning and serve.

CHEFS NOTE
Adjust the amount of Tabasco sauce to suit your own taste, and add a little more olive oil if it needs loosening up.

BORLOTTI BEAN PUREE

195
calories per
serving

Ingredients

- 1 lemon
- 300g/11oz tinned borlotti beans, drained
- 1 tsp freshly chopped rosemary

- 1 garlic clove, crushed
- 2 tbsp olive oil
- Salt & pepper to taste

Method

1 First grate the zest off the lemon. Juice the remainder of the lemon and discard the flesh. Add the lemon zest and juice to a food processor along with all the other ingredients. Pulse until smooth. Season and serve.

CHEFS NOTE
A few flakes of dried crushed chillies make a good garnish to this simple dip.

CAPER & OLIVE TAPENADE

85
calories per serving

Ingredients

- 200g/7oz black olives
- 2 tbsp capers
- 1 garlic clove
- 4 tbsp freshly chopped flat leaf parsley
- 2 tbsp olive oil
- Salt & pepper to taste

Method

1 Make sure the olives are pitted. Add all the ingredients to a food processor and pulse until smooth. Adjust the seasoning and serve with a drizzle of olive oil over the top and a little black pepper.

CHEFS NOTE

This is great as a topping on rye bread. If you are a fan of anchovies try adding a couple of tinned fillets to give a further dimension to the flavour.

SOYA BEAN DIP

220 calories per serving

Ingredients

- 400g/14oz frozen soya beans
- 2 tbsp Greek yoghurt
- 1 garlic clove, crushed
- ½ red chilli, deseeded and finely chopped
- 2 shallots, finely chopped
- 2 tbsp freshly chopped mint
- 1 tbsp lime juice
- 2 tbsp olive oil
- Splash of water
- Salt & pepper to taste

Method

1 Cook the soya beans in boiling water, drain and leave to cool for a few minutes.

2 Add all the ingredients to a food processor and pulse until the beans have lost their form but still have a coarseness - this shouldn't be a completely smooth dip. Add a little water if it needs loosening up. Allow it to cool, season and serve.

CHEFS NOTE
You could substitute the mint in this recipe for fresh coriander.

AUBERGINE & FETA DIP

175 calories per serving

Ingredients

- 3 large aubergines/egg plant
- 2 garlic cloves, crushed
- 2 tbsp freshly chopped oregano or basil
- 2 tbsp lemon juice
- 2 tbsp olive oil
- 75g/3oz feta cheese
- Splash of water
- Salt & pepper to taste

Method

1 Preheat the oven to 200C/400F/Gas Mark 6

2 Slice the aubergines in half lengthways and roast flesh-side down in a preheated oven for 20-30 minutes or until tender. Scoop the flesh out of the skins and place in a food processor along with the garlic, oregano, lemon juice, olive oil and feta cheese. Pulse until smooth and add a little water if needed to loosen it up. Allow it to cool, season and serve.

CHEFS NOTE

Add some fresh chives or mint to this dip if you wish. Serve with vegetable crudités.

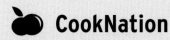 CookNation

Other COOKNATION TITLES

If you enjoyed **The Skinny Blood Sugar Diet Recipe Book** you may also be interested in other great cookbooks in the CookNation series including our range of **5:2 Fast Diet** recipe books.

You can browse all titles at www.bellmackenzie.com

Thank you.